In the Sun

Explorer Challenge

Who is dressed for the
wrong weather?

OXFORD

UNIVERSITY PRESS

2

Retell the Story

Look at the pictures and retell the story in your own words.

Look Back, Explorers

What happened to
Dad's feet?

The family played in the
sand at the beach. What
other things could they
have done?

What are Biff and Chip
holding on page 6?

Did you find out
who was dressed
for the wrong
weather?

Explorer Challenge: a man wearing boots, rain hat
and raincoat, and carrying an umbrella (page 2)

What's Next, Explorers?

Now find out what to wear in different kinds of weather ...

Explorer Challenge for
Sun Hat, Sunscreen, Sun!

What are these people doing?